A
REFRESHING
CHUCKLE

Twenty-Six Empowering Devotionals
to Overcome the Oppressiveness of
Shame, Guilt and Regret

DR. CHUCK GLENN

Dr. Chuck Glenn
Momentswithyahweh@gmail.com
Lincoln, Nebraska

Visit us on Facebook @MomentswithYahweh

DEDICATION

No book is written by one individual, it takes a small army to bring a concept to publication. I hope I have included everyone involved in this project. If I have missed anyone, please forgive me. For: Philana, who challenged me to take my creative writing skills and use them for the LORD; Jeff, who read more than his share of these devotionals with an eye toward providing constructive guidance; the Nebraska Department of Correctional Services Religion Study Committee whose members encouraged me as I tentatively stepped out to write this book and who put up with more than their fair share of puns; Daryl, my accountability partner who meets with me most Saturday mornings for fast food and has been involved in talking through all phases of this book; Pastor Cleve Smith, who helped me understand supporting people as they grow in their spiritual life is just as important as writing deep theological-based Bible studies; Chris, Charity, Shanda, Trina, and Brooke for helping me to become a better father; Bell, who provided more than a couple of the puns found in this book; Rick and Vickie, who took three weeks out of their busy schedule to read through the entire book and provided clear and direct feedback; the team at Just Write Communications without whose help this book would have never seen print; Zeny, my Proverbs 31 wife, who saw my fear of rejection, stood beside me as I struggled to write from a place behind my carefully crafted walls, and who painstakingly worked behind the scenes to bring this book to life; and most importantly to my LORD and Savior Jesus Christ, who died that I might live, leaving this earth to sit at the right hand of the Father, making way for the Holy Spirit, who has given me a tremendous spiritual gift and talents galore to go along with it.

FORWARD

It had been months since I caught up with Chuck. We no longer worked down the hall from each other and it had been a while since I said, "Have a good evening" as I left our office building. I was usually the *second* person to leave, so I don't really know how long Chuck remained working after I left.

I was eager to know how he had been and what was percolating in that gifted noggin of his. So, I was understandably cautious when he announced that he was on the verge of completing his new book on pun devotionals. *Pun Devotionals.* My visible reaction was practiced, unconditional affirmation—the kind you develop after spending a few decades managing adversity while smiling. But inside my head, I was shouting, "Are you *Crazy*?" Nonetheless, I smiled, nodded and determined to listen to the whole of his kooky enterprise without judgement. Chuck explained the book would introduce a pun and provide a related message of hope, redemption, and possibilities to the reader. I was breathing a little easier now because I trusted this man. In addition to his multi-faceted expertise in comparative religions and thorough theological training, Chuck is a devoted husband, friend, and ambassador of the love and grace of Jesus Christ. His humor, quality of character, and friendship make it an honor to write this forward.

So, here is his book. Its contents reflect the depth, sincerity, cerebral mass, and sense of humor unique to Chuck Glenn. In reading it, you will either scoff or groan at the puns and settle in to reading the insight, wisdom, and true value of Chuck's considerable education, devotion, and experience. You will be enriched, affirmed, illuminated, and challenged.

Mike Kenney
Director, Nebraska Department of Correctional Services (Retired)
July 2019

Pun Statistic:

A contest was put forth for those who write puns.
After submission, the puns were to undergo a rigorous scrutiny to see if they qualified to get into Chuck's book.
Because of the harsh standards, only ten puns were submitted.

Did any of these puns make the cut?

No pun in ten did.

INTRODUCTION

I love a great pun and for me, a good pun causes me to silently groan or chuckle out loud (my belief is that a silent groan is as good as a chuckle out loud). This book is unique, in that every devotion starts with a pun, allowing each of us the opportunity to chuckle as we begin our day. I've also tried to be honest and transparent about my struggles with the topic discussed in each devotion, which will hopefully allow you, the reader, to know you are not alone in your struggles.

All of us fail, and all of us have times we are battered by the shame, guilt, and regret those failures bring. God's plan is to provide His children freedom from the oppression experienced through shame, guilt, or regret. My hope for you as you read this book is you will begin to experience the freedom that our LORD provides His children.

There are a couple of ways this book can be used. You can read one devotional a day for twenty-six days, or get together with a small informal group of friends each week. However you decide to use it, be sure to read though the questions in the "Digging Deeper" sections.

I would like to leave you with one of my favorite verses in the Old Testament.

"The Lord bless you and keep you; the Lord make his face shine on you and be gracious to you; the Lord turn his face toward you and give you peace."

Numbers 6:24-26

Chuck Glenn
Lincoln, NE

Where did Captain Hook buy his hook?

At a second hand store.

TABLE OF CONTENTS

PAST TENTS

Why can't you run through a campground?
You can only ran because it's past tents.

As I read that pun, I began to think of my past and I have to admit there are many parts of it I want to run away from. It seems the older I get, the more I regret actions of my past. I am hounded at times with the thoughts of what I've said to other people, the way I've treated friends and family, and my actions with those within the Christian community. I have struggled for years with these feelings, wondering if my future held restoration and peace.

I finally had the courage to share my feelings within a group of Christian men I trust. I was shocked to find each of them struggled with the same thing at times. Knowing that other people struggled with their past helped, but it did not bring the restoration I desperately wanted. The LORD led me to Isaiah chapter forty-three.

In this chapter, the LORD is speaking through Isaiah and comforts His people who are currently under Babylonian rule. Verse one reads, "But now, this is what the LORD says—he who created you, Jacob, he who formed you, Israel: "Do not fear, for I have redeemed you; I have summoned you by name; you are mine."

There are a lot of great promises in this verse, but I want to focus on three. First, God reminds the people of Israel He is the one who created them. Second, because He created them, He knows them so deeply He calls them by name. Third, He tells His people they belong to Him. The underlying thought in this verse is: God knows me to the depth of my being and in spite of my flaws, He claims me for His own.

Although verse one tells me I am God's and He claims me for His own, it does not bring about hope and restoration. I found the hope and restoration I was seeking deeper within the text in verses eighteen and nineteen. Isaiah writes, "Forget the former things; do not dwell on the past. See, I am doing a new thing! Now it springs up; do you not perceive it? I am making a way in the wilderness and streams in the wasteland."

Here is what God tells me to do. First, forget the former things and do not consider the things of the past. Second, recognize God is doing a new work in me and I need to focus on what he is doing, not what I have done. When I do this, He promises to make a path in the wilderness, where I struggle with hope and restoration. The road clearly leads out of the wilderness where I have thirst for release from the past. Then He promises restoration by providing life-giving water along the way.

God has provided a road and life-giving water to bring me out of my wilderness filled with the remembrance of former actions, failures, and defeats. The message is clear, God calls out and says "Forget the past. Come walk with me and be restored." I am going to accept His offer.

Digging Deeper

1) Do you struggle with things from the past? Please explain.
2) How will focusing on what God is doing give you hope and restoration?
3) What obstacles do you foresee in preventing you from focusing on God's path?
4) How can members of the group you are meeting with support you?

COUPLES WORKOUT

Why don't more couples go to the gym?
Because some relationships don't work out.

I've had a lot of different relationships during my life. There have been girlfriends, friends, and people I considered intimate friends. Most of those relationships didn't work out. I lost my best friend from childhood when I was a senior in high school because I was a jerk. I remember sitting in my room and crying over my stupidity. The worst part of the situation was the bridge I burned because there was no hope of restoring that relationship.

As I think about George (not his real name) and my failure, my mind jumps to thoughts about God. I have failed in my relationship with Him more times than I want to remember. I have a habit of wandering away from Him, yet I tell Him I love Him. If God were a human friend, He would have walked away from me and never looked back because of the way I've treated Him. But God's relationship with me is not built on human love or understanding. It is built on His grace.

When I think I have ruined my relationship with God by deliberately walking into sin, I often times read Isaiah 43:25 and am amazed at God's response to my actions. This verse tells me God does the exact opposite of what I expect. It tells

4

me that He blots out my transgressions and remembers my sin no more. I find that amazing! I purposely choose to do wrong, but God chooses to restore the relationship! In 1 John 1:9 we are told how this occurs. The forgiveness and blotting out of my transgression happens when I come before God with true sorrow for what I've done and seek forgiveness. When I do this, He forgives me and remembers my sin no more.

My relationship with God rests on this fact: there is nothing I can do to make God love me more than He does and there is nothing I can do to make Him love me less than He does. It is an unbreakable relationship that works out because of His love, mercy, and grace.

Are you like me? Do you find it easier to believe God is angry at you for deliberately walking into sin? If so, why not join me as I learn to accept the forgiving relationship with a being who loved me so much, He sent His only Son to die for those sins I deliberately step into? "This is how God showed His love among us; He sent his one and only Son into the world that we might live through Him." (1 John 4:9)

Digging Deeper

1) Have you ever felt like God should turn His back on you because of deliberately choosing to walk into sin? Please explain.
2) 1 John 1:8 tells us that anyone who says they do not sin is a liar. Explain why you agree or disagree.

3) 1 John 1:9 tells us when we confess our sin to God; He will forgive us and cleanse us. Do you believe this? Why or why not?
4) How can members of the group you are meeting with support you?

AVOID THE OYSTERS

Avoid the Oysters.
They will make you feel clammy.

When I tell my wife I feel clammy, she knows I mean I'm not feeling well physically. However, if I was truthful, I would have to admit there are times I don't feel very good about my relationship with God. Typically, those are the times when I feel God has abandoned me. One of my hardest struggles came when my friend Marvin (not his real name) died. Marvin's liver began to fail. Many members in my church prayed that he would be healed or he would get a liver transplant. Our prayers were answered and within a few weeks, he received a new liver. We prayed for a quick recovery, but that did not happen. His liver began to fail, and I prayed constantly. Marvin had a wife who adored and loved him, along with a son who had recently graduated from high school. I begged God to heal Marvin, but he continued to go downhill. Then came the day I received the dreaded call. Marvin had been admitted to the hospital with complete liver failure. I prayed and began fasting, crying, and begging God to heal my friend. After a few days God took Marvin home. I have never felt so abandoned by God! I knew without a doubt Marvin loved God, and trusted in him, yet God let him die. God did not answer my prayer the way I needed Him to answer. God failed me.

I took Philippians 4:6 to heart and I let God have it. In the New Living Translation this verse is translated like this, "Don't worry about anything; instead, pray about everything. Tell God what you need, and thank him for all he has done." I told Him about everything. I expressed my anger, disappointment, feelings of abandonment, and how He had failed me. God, in His gentle way showed me Psalm 22:6-14. In this passage, David is addressing God the same way I did. He shows respect, but he also empties his heart out to the LORD. As we move through this psalm, we find that David comes to a point where he begins to remember what God has done in the past and in remembering, knows that God has not abandoned him. David realizes God is right there with him in the heartache, pain, and disappointment.

I don't know why God did not answer my prayers for Marvin the way I wanted Him to. I still hurt and miss my friend. Yet I know God walks beside me and has never failed to take care of or watch over me. Having this knowledge and feeling his presence allows me to trust Him and His plan. The next time I feel God has abandoned me, I need call to mind David's example in Psalm 22 and reach out in honest humbleness to God. The answer may not be what I want, but I know God will answer, and he will be by my side.

Digging Deeper

1) Please re-read Psalm twenty-two verses six through eleven. How does the focus of verses six through eight

differ when compared to the focus of verses nine through eleven?

2) What do verses nine through eleven teach us about the presence of God when we feel like He has abandoned us?

3) What are some steps you can take to remember Psalm 22 the next time you feel abandoned by God?

4) How can members of the group you are meeting with support you?

COFFEE GOT MUGGED

Why did the coffee file a police report?
It got mugged.

I love coffee, but I've noticed as I have gotten older, I have to be careful about drinking caffeinated coffee after about 2 p.m. When I do, I am up all night and am pretty much worthless the next day. That's why I am so thankful for decaffeinated coffee. It allows me to experience the smell and taste of coffee after 2 p.m. and I have no trouble falling asleep. Two types of coffee with two different effects on my body.

This makes me think of two different types of wisdom I am afforded, and the role each type of wisdom plays in my life. The wisdom of this world and the wisdom of God. I like the way James explains this in chapter three of his letter. Starting in verse thirteen he writes, "Who is wise and understanding among you? Let them show it by their good life, by deeds done in the humility that comes from wisdom." Verse sixteen tells us the result of earthly wisdom. It is disorder and the emergence of evil things. Galatians chapter five tells us what those earthly things are: sexual immorality, impurity, sensuality, idolatry, sorcery, enmity, strife, jealously, fits of anger, rivalries, dissensions, divisions, envy, drunkenness, and partying in a drunken manner.

On the other hand, James tell us the wisdom from above is pure, peaceful, gentle, reasonable, full of mercy, good fruits, impartial, and sincere. In Galatians five verses twenty-two through twenty-three, Paul tells us the result of God's wisdom. It is love, joy, peace, patience, kindness, goodness, faithfulness, gentleness, and self-control. The question I have to ask myself each day is this: which person do I want to be, the one Paul describes in Galatians 5:19-21, brought about by the wisdom of the world or the one written about in verses 22-23, brought about by God's wisdom?

To be a person who bears good fruit, I must choose wisdom from above. When I drink coffee after 2 p.m. I have a choice regarding which type of coffee I will feed my body, caffeinated or decaffeinated. When I look for wisdom, I have a choice regarding which type I will feed myself, the world's or God's. If I want to bear God's fruit, I must choose wisdom from above. The source of wisdom from which I feed myself will determine who I become. It is difficult to follow God's path of wisdom, but it is worth my effort. As G.K. Chesterton said, "Christianity has not been tried and found wanting, it has been found difficult and left untried." I have chosen the difficult path of wisdom given by God and strive to bypass the easier wisdom of the world. Although I am not always successful in choosing Gods wisdom, I try hard. When I fail, I come before Him in brokenness and humbleness asking for His forgiveness which He freely gives. I invite you to join me in this effort.

Digging Deeper

1) What do you feed your mind? More of Gods wisdom or more of the world's wisdom?
2) Do you agree with G.K. Chesterton's statement? Why or why not?
3) What steps can you take to begin to feed your mind more of God's wisdom?
4) How can members of the group you are meeting with support you?

BACKFLIP

Did I tell you about the time I fell in love
during a backflip?
I was heels overhead.

I didn't fall in love during a back flip, but I did fall in love with an amazing lady. One thing I know about myself is I have a deep desire to take care of the love of my life. I want to tend to her and make sure I am doing everything I can to meet her needs.

The writer in Proverbs speaks about tending to a fig tree. Now I have to admit, I've never fallen in love with a fig tree let alone loving one the way I love my wife, but the writer of Proverbs 27:18 has a point when he writes, "The one who guards a fig tree will eat its fruit, and whoever protects their master will be honored." I don't believe the author is speaking about a literal fig tree. I believe he is using a fig tree to help the reader understand that just as a fig tree needs tending, so do various aspects of our lives. The fig tree could apply to our relationship with our spouse, our physical health, or our emotional state. I like to apply this proverb to my spiritual life.

In Old Testament times, people who owned fig trees gave them daily care. They made sure the tree was fertilized, watered, and pruned so that it would bear fruit and feed their family. My spiritual life needs the same care each and every day. The question is how do I water, fertilize, and prune my spiritual life? One way to do this is to set aside ten minutes, three times a day. I'm not suggesting that a person set aside thirty minutes at one time, I'm suggesting that three times a day, a person take ten minutes to do three specific things. During the first ten minutes read through a chapter of Proverbs and make a short, one sentence note about a verse that grabs your attention or makes you think. This is how we fertilize our spiritual life, we read God's word and let it sink into our lives so that it will provide us insight for times of joy, trouble, and stress. During the next ten-minute break, approach God in prayer. This is how we water our spiritual life. We talk with God. One of my favorite verses is Philippians 4:6, which reads, "Do not be anxious about anything, but in every situation, by prayer and petition, with thanksgiving, present your requests to God." The best part of that verse is the word "everything." Define everything. Nothing is off limits to talk to God about. My inability to overcome sin, my anger at God, it's all included in the word everything. So, take ten minutes and just talk to Him. During your last ten-minute break, work on memorizing a Bible verse. Don't worry about how long it takes you to memorize it, just work on it every day for ten minutes until you have it down. Once you have it memorized, pick another one to work on. This is how we prune our lives.

Scripture has a habit of helping us to see the path we need to be on compared to the path we are on. When we choose to walk the path scripture points to, we begin to prune away the world's influence in our lives. Ten minutes three times a day will fertilize, water, and prune our spiritual lives much like the Old Testament individual fertilized, watered, and pruned his fig tree. When this is done, we mature in Christ and in turn are able to produce fruit for Him, which in turn feeds others. Why not try three tens today?

Digging Deeper

1) What would keep you from committing to three by ten each day?
2) Will you commit to three by ten for a week, month, year?
3) What obstacles do you foresee in preventing you from keeping your commitment?
4) How can members of the group you are meeting with support you?

PIANO IN A MINESHAFT

Show me a piano falling down a mine shaft and I'll show you A-flat minor.

Have you ever felt like the life you are living is flat? Especially when it comes to your spiritual life? I have. There have been times I have felt defeated by my inability to step away from temptations and I feel like a failure, especially if I continue to fall to one particular temptation. When I experience that, I feel spiritually flat, like I need to get a handle on myself and the sin I'm locked into before I can approach God.

Yet, what I think I need to do is exactly opposite of what the writer of Proverbs 9:4-6 tells us to do. He writes, "Let all who are simple come to my house!' To those who have no sense she says, 'Come, eat my food and drink the wine I have mixed. Leave your simple ways and you will live; walk in the way of insight.'" In these verses God is personified as wisdom. Many times, when He calls, we think our disheveled, sinful, desperate lives need to be put in order before we can accept His way, yet this text tells us something different.

Look at the steps the author under the direction of the Holy Spirit lays out for us. First, we come, then we eat and drink, then we recognize our ways, after that we walk. God

16

invites us as we are to fellowship with him, before we begin to continue on the path He has for us. After we come, eat and drink, he invites us to walk His path.

The message is clear, we are to come as we are, eat, drink, then walk with the LORD. I've decided to take this offer, how about joining me?

Digging Deeper

1) Have you ever felt so spiritually flat you did not think God could use you? If so, please explain.
2) If you no longer feel that way, explain what happened. If you feel that way now, what will you do?
3) How can members of the group you are meeting with support you?

ALMOND DIET

I thought about going on an all-almond diet, but
that would be just nuts.

I used to think that the word "diet" was nothing more than
the word "die" with a "t" added on the end. I thought, "Who
needs those things?" Then I got older and my metabolism
slowed down. Next came the biological fact that it takes
longer to recover from a hard workout than it did ten years
ago. The end result of all of the above is my waist line has
grown and now the word diet has become a functional part
of my vocabulary.

In the third chapter of Ecclesiastes, the writer tells us that
there is an appointed time for every event under heaven, like
going on a diet, or revamping the intensity of my workouts.
In verse one, he writes, "There is a time for everything, and
a season for every activity under the heavens." If there is an
appointed time for everything and every event this would
also include my spiritual life as well.

When I think of that I have to ask myself, how am I doing
at setting up time to grow in my spiritual life? To be honest,
there have been times that I am embarrassed to answer that
question. At times I have allowed other things to become far
more important in my life than spiritual growth. I have
allowed myself to read books of fiction instead of being in

God's word. I have spent time on the golf course when I should have been spending time on my knees praying. Neither of those activities are wrong, I just did them at the wrong time.

I was trying to explain this to a person I was golfing with, and his response was, "I don't read the Bible. If I have a spiritual question about anything, I just come to you, or ask one of the pastors at church." The truth is all of us neglect our spiritual growth at times. We do that because we are flawed human beings and we give into the temptations the world offers. For me its fictional books and golf.

Yet in Ecclesiastes 3:11 the writer makes a pertinent statement. He writes, "...He has also set eternity in the human heart..." I like how Albert Barnes speaks about this in his theological volume titled Barnes' Notes on Ecclesiastes, "God has placed in the inborn constitution of man the capability of conceiving of eternity, the struggle to apprehend the everlasting, the longing after an eternal life."[1] This means that no matter how often I turn to reading my books or go golfing, I am aware of the calling to turn to God, to experience more of him, and draw closer to Him. Hearing God means I place reading and golf in their proper place, and give my LORD the time He deserves. My challenge to you is to join me in committing to give God the time He deserves.

Digging Deeper

1) What activities do you allow to pull you away from time with God?

---

[1] Albert Barnes, Barnes Notes on the Old Testament, Ecclesiastes 3:11, BibleHub.com, accessed February 19, 2019.

2) How has this effected your spiritual growth?
3) What steps will you take in order to give God the time He deserves?
4) How can members of the group you are meeting with support you?

BLINDSIDED

Two men walked into a bar.
The second one should have seen it coming.

That second man was blindsided by the bar. He should have seen it coming, but he didn't. Have you ever been blindsided? I think back to the time I was pastoring at a church and was befriended by a member of the congregation. He encouraged me to share with him personal doubts, fears, and struggles. Little did I know he was taking everything I said back to other members of the church. As word spread about what I said to him, the stories became distorted and he made no effort to correct them even though he knew the truth. Not only did he speak about my private matters, but he let lies go unchecked. All of this was done behind by back. I found out about it when I was asked to leave the church. I was blindsided.

I feel I sometimes do the same thing to God. It seems that one moment I can be deeply engaged in pouring my heart out to Him in prayer and experience a feeling of closeness with Him I can never give voice to, then a short time later I blindside Him by doing the very action I so recently spent time in prayer about. It seems to me I cozy up to God and once I feel his forgiveness, warmth, and acceptance, I go out and blindside Him with my words or actions. I often wonder how God can use me in His work because of my actions.

The good news is God is not blindsided by my actions. He knows me to the very core of my being. One of my favorite scriptures describes this in Psalm 139:1-4, "You have searched me, Lord, and you know me. You know when I sit and when I rise; you perceive my thoughts from afar. You discern my going out and my lying down; you are familiar with all my ways. Before a word is on my tongue you, Lord, know it completely." Further on, in verses thirteen through sixteen, David writes that the LORD formed our inward parts, our frame was not hidden from him and that His eyes have seen our unformed substance.

When I read Psalm 139, I take comfort in David's writing. I see that God has searched me, and is intimately familiar with who and what I am. God knows what I am going to say before I say it. I think it's pretty hard to blindside someone who knows what is coming. But the real beauty of this verse is what it means to me. God knows that I will intimately seek him in prayer and desire his forgiveness, warmth, and acceptance. He also knows I will leave that time of prayer and, despite my best intentions, I will fail Him in word, action, or deed—sometimes all three. Yet He accepts me and loves me unconditionally because I am His child. I can't blindside God.

Are you buying into the thought you are not acceptable to Christ because of what you have done in your past? Maybe you have believed the inward lies you have told yourself regarding your inability to serve because of your failures. However, the truth is just the opposite. In spite of everything we have done, Christ accepts us and forgives unconditionally. Nothing we have done or will do is a surprise to Him. Why not approach Him in humbleness, ask for and receive His forgiveness, then let Him use you to further His kingdom on earth?

Digging Deeper

1) What actions or situations from your past or present do you struggle with?
2) Do you believe God knows about these and has forgiven them? Why or why not?
3) Knowing that God forgives, what is stopping you from being used by Him?
4) How can members of the group you are meeting with support you?

GLUE STICK/CHAPSTICK

I accidentally handed my wife a glue stick instead
of a chap stick.
She still isn't talking to me.

There are times I wish someone had used a glue stick on my mouth. It seems I need it most when someone wants to correct me. I don't hear anyone giving me constructive criticism, I just hear criticism and I want to defend myself. Yet the Bible tells us proper criticism (called instruction) is necessary in order to gain understanding and wisdom.

The book of Proverbs is full of verses which encourage us to heed instruction and let it affect our lives. One of my favorites is Proverbs 8:33, "Listen to my instruction and be wise; do not disregard it." The Hebrew word for "listen" is *shama*. We know it is important to this verse because the way *shama* is used indicates the action is an authoritative command. This tells us we need to hear instruction and take heed of it, placing it within the very essence of our being.

At times, even when I know I need to take in instruction, I still balk at accepting it. That's when the verse I love to hate begins to echo through my thoughts. It's Proverbs 13:18 and has become a life verse for me. It reads, "Whoever disregards discipline comes to poverty and shame, but whoever heeds correction is honored." Very few of us like this instruction and to be honest I don't know of anyone who jumps out of bed and yells "Reprove me! Please reprove me!" Yet God's instruction, as painful as it may be, always leads us to His presence and there we find strength, comfort, and peace in the midst of instruction and reproof.

Digging Deeper

1) Do you find instruction and correction difficult to deal with? Why or Why not?
2) How will you deal with instruction and correction the next time one of them happens to you?
3) Would memorizing Proverbs 13:18 help you when you find yourself being reproved or instructed?
4) How can members of the group you are meeting with support you?

MILK STOOL

Why does a milk stool only have three legs?
Because the cow has the utter.

For me, what makes this pun funny is the rhyme between the word "utter" and the implied word "other." There have been times in my life when the events that occur makes no sense to me. Prayer is one of the events that makes no sense. Philippians 4:6 tells me to bring everything to God. I firmly believe this means God desires for me to tell Him everything (when I quote this verse I usually say "define everything").

There are times I have emptied my heart out to the Lord in prayer and He answers them either through direct results or scripture, but there are other times I pray and it seems that God is silent or that He just isn't interested in what I have to say. When I come to the point where God's reaction to my prayer makes no sense, I turn to Habakkuk 3:17-18.

Habakkuk does not understand why God is going to allow His nation to be invaded by a people group who are far worse than Israel. Yet through his interaction with Yahweh, Habakkuk came to understand the only thing he needed to do was to rely on God and not his own wisdom. Here is his prayer:

Though the fig tree should not blossom
  And there be no fruit on the vines,
  Though the yield of the olive should fail
  And the fields produce no food,
  Though the flock should be cut off from the fold
  And there be no cattle in the stalls,

Yet I will exalt in the LORD,
  I will rejoice in the God of my salvation.
The Lord GOD is my strength,
  And He has made my feet like hinds' feet,
  And makes me walk on my high places.
  For the choir director, on my stringed instruments.

If you are like me and struggle with God's silence or with the direction God is leading your life, why not join Habakkuk in knowing God hears you and more importantly wants the best for you. I have found the best way to do this is to be honest with God and tell Him exactly what my struggles are. He gives me strength by helping me to embrace the Holy Spirit inside me. Things seldom get better overnight, yet I have a peace which calms me in spite of the stalls being empty. Why not join me as I journey toward trusting God even though my fig tree may not bloom?

Digging Deeper

1) Do you or have you struggled with thinking God does not hear your prayer? Please explain.
2) Read all three chapters of Habakkuk. Why do you think Habakkuk was able to pray his prayer in 3:17-18?

3) How can you apply this to your life?
4) How can members of the group you are meeting with support you?

TOUCAN

A friend of mine tried to annoy me with bird puns,
but I soon realized toucan play that game.

I remember more than a few times when I've said, "Oh
yeah, two can play that game." Then followed thoughts of
revenge and planning in order to get back at someone. To
my shame, I actually followed through on a couple of those.
Years later I apologized, but that doesn't change the fact I
did it.

There is a great story in the Bible about the opportunity
to extract revenge on some people and how the person who
was mistreated handled what happened. The story is found
in Genesis chapters 37-45. Let me set the stage for you.
Joseph's brothers sold him into slavery and then lied to their
father about what happened to him. They lead Jacob,
Joseph's father, to believe Joseph had been killed by a wild
animal. Joseph ends up in Egypt and becomes a very
powerful individual within the Egyptian government. A
severe famine breaks out in Egypt and the surrounding
nations. There is no food to be found except in Egypt.
Jacob's family begins to run short on grain so he sends his
sons to Egypt to get more. Unknown to them, Joseph is in
charge of all the warehouses holding the grain and for this
reason his brothers are brought before him. He recognizes

them, but because he is now a mature man, the brothers do not recognize him. Can you imagine what it would be like to be a man of power in your nation and have the ones who sold you into slavery kneeling before you? Joseph has his brother's lives in his hands. Yet he does not give into hate, but instead goes through a process which results in his brothers receiving his forgiveness along with Pharaoh allowing his family to move to Egypt and giving them the best of the land in Egypt.

How was Joseph able to forgive? My belief is it began with the ability to dwell on forgiving his brothers, not hating them. If he had chosen to hate them, he would have pounced on the opportunity to pay them back one hundred times over. I think each time he thought about them, he had to ask God for the strength to forgive them. Christ did the same thing when He was hung on the cross. He had been deserted by His closest friends, lied about, and horribly beaten. Yet He called on His Father to forgive mankind. This kind of forgiveness is what Paul stresses in Ephesians 4:32. He writes, "Be kind and compassionate to one another, forgiving each other, just as in Christ God forgave you."

I still struggle with thoughts of revenge at times, but I know I'm not the only one who does so. When I do, I think of Joseph and what Paul wrote in Ephesians, then I ask for forgiveness and the strength to forgive. This is a journey for me. Will you join me?

Digging Deeper

1) Is there someone or a group of individuals you struggle to forgive? Why?

2) Knowing that forgiveness is a difficult journey, what are some steps you can take to begin and continue the process?
3) How can members of the group you are meeting with support you?

HIPPO AND ZIPPO

What is the difference between a Hippo
and a Zippo?
One is really heavy, the other is
a little lighter.

Being lighthearted is something I struggle with because I
tend to let the seriousness of life overshadow my joy.

I love how the writer of Ecclesiastes speaks about this
problem. In chapter three verse one he writes, "There is a
time for everything, and a season for every activity under the
heavens:" The author then provides a list of opposites such
as in verse two where he writes, "a time to be born and a time
to die, a time to plant and a time to uproot," In verse four he
writes, "a time to weep and a time to laugh, a time to mourn
and a time to dance." In other words, there is time to be light
and a time to be heavy.

When my mother lost her battle with a bad heart and the
LORD took her home, I experienced a sorrow and heaviness
which sank into the very depths of my being. The lady who
was my nurse, confidant, driving coach, and one of my
encouragers while I pursued my doctorate was no longer
alive. I would never again hear her laughter or her affirming
words, "Charlie, don't quit, I believe in you." Yet her death
was a time of great rejoicing for me. No longer was the lady

who climbed cliffs with me and played hockey against me, confined to a walker and an oxygen tank, she was free at last. In the midst of the soul wrenching sorrow and heaviness, a peace that is beyond understanding flooded my being. My mom was free!

An amazing thing happened to me that day, happiness and joy came to a point of co-existence inside of me. There was seriousness in her death, but by remembering our joyful experiences as I watched her cold, unmoving body lifted on a gurney, rolled out to a waiting hearse, loaded and driven out of site, joy bubbled within me. In Psalm 126:1-3 we read that those who have been brought back from captivity are filled with rejoicing. At the same time, verses four through six show sorrow for the captives who have not been given freedom.

A time to weep and a time to laugh. A time to be lighthearted and a time to be heavy. Rejoicing even in sorrow is not easy, yet as we commit to it, we find the LORD walks beside us.

Digging Deeper

1) Do you sometimes struggle to be lighthearted? Why or why not?
2) What are some joyful memories from your past?
3) List four joyful times you have spent with God.
4) How can members of the group you are meeting with support you?

HOW DOES A PENGUIN BUILD A HOUSE?

How does a penguin build a house?
Igloos it together.

I grew up in South Dakota and during winter, Mother Nature provided a considerable amount of snow with which my brother and I made a lot of igloos, or at least attempted to. Our igloos were imperfect to say the least. They weren't circular, in fact I'm not sure there is a word that can describe some of the shapes we ended up building. Yet for us they were perfect! Each one we built was unique. Some were forts, others were hideouts, and still others were shelter from the cold and wind. One thing was for certain, no matter what the shape or the function, each one was crafted with care.

I'm built the same way. In Psalms 139:14, David writes, "I praise you because I am fearfully and wonderfully made; your works are wonderful; I know that full well." Although I know God has made me, I struggle with who I am. Sometimes when a picture is taken of me, I look at it and think my ears make me look like a taxi, headed down the street with a door on either side open. Then there is the issue of my non-athletic ability. I'm the guy on his football team that played end, guard, and tackle at the same time. I sat on the end of the bench, guarded the water bucket, and tackled anyone who tried to get a drink. I haven't even gotten to my thoughts and my spiritual life. I look at myself and I think I'm a wreck. Yet that is not the truth. I am not a wreck; I am fearfully and wonderfully made by the one who spoke the universe into existence.

The word "fearfully" in Hebrew carries the idea of the wonderful, glorious things of Yahweh Himself. The word "wonderful" means to be separate or distinct. In other words, this Psalm tells me the God who spoke the universe into existence made me glorious and distinct!

If I look at myself from that perspective, I see a different person, one who the LORD has given an inquisitive mind driven to research until a credible answer is found. He also gave me great organizational skills and an unquenchable thirst for His word. I am fearfully and wonderfully made! The real question is how will I choose to view myself? Am I an igloo that is built so strange there isn't a name for my shape, or am I unique, designed for a special purpose? How will you choose to view yourself from this day forward?

Digging Deeper

1) How do you view yourself? Are you an igloo designed for a special purpose or a misshaped heap of snow? Why?
2) What are some of your unique gifts and talents?
3) How can you use those in God's work?
4) How can members of the group you are meeting with support you?

PATIENCE

Why did the doctor have to retire?
Because he ran out of patience.

One thing I've learned in life is if I am hungry or tired, I easily run out of patience. When I think of being fed, I think of Proverbs 30:8. It reads, "Keep falsehood and lies far from me; give me neither poverty nor riches, but give me only my daily bread." A closer translation of the last part of that verse, "...but give me only my daily bread," would be "...feed me with the food allotted to me." Although the author of this proverb, a man named Agur, is clearly speaking about physical food, this verse often strikes me as being about spiritual food.

I have to admit until I began to study Agur's writing, I had never thought of asking the LORD to feed me spiritually. I often ask for the LORD to guide me as I work through a scripture passage, but I have never asked, "LORD would you feed my spirit today with what you want me to learn and apply to my life?"

You see, my natural tendency is to be mean, self-seeking, jealous, and angry. To counteract this, I need to ask to be given the right portion of spiritual food. I don't want to be stuffed and I don't want to starve spiritually, I want the proper portion in order to be effective in bringing my spiritual life into physical existence. The way the Hebrew word "feed" is used in this verse leads me to believe Agur wanted the act of being fed to be an ongoing action. However, the action indicated is not one of complete fulfillment, but rather of continually receiving the portion needed each day to keep from being hungry. In the same way I need to ask the LORD to feed me the portion needed each day to live a life which reflects Christ's virtues— not those I naturally tend toward.

There is a spiritual war inside of me between my natural tendencies and Christ's virtues. When I face this warfare, 2 Corinthians 10:4-5 provides me with help. It says, "The weapons we fight with are not the weapons of the world. On the contrary, they have divine power to demolish strongholds. We demolish arguments and every pretension that sets itself up against the knowledge of God, and we take captive every thought to make it obedient to Christ." Praying to be fed my right portion of spiritual food means I will acquire the spiritual weapons I need in order to assure that I win the spiritual war going on inside of me. This is not an easy task, but it is one that I am asking each of you to commit to doing with me.

Digging Deeper

1) Is there a tension inside of you between your spiritual man and your earthly man? If so describe one of the tension (or spiritual warfare) points.

2) List your spiritual weapons below and share them with your group.

3) How can members of the group you are meeting with support you?

TIRED BICYCLE

Why couldn't the bicycle stand up by itself?
It was two-tired.

Have you ever been so tired you felt you couldn't stand up? Maybe you're a college student and it's the last day of finals, or work is so stressful and busy it seems to drain every ounce of energy out of you. When I think of the times, I've been too tired to stand, overwhelmed by issues I felt I had no control over, it felt like I was in deep water without hope of rescue. David felt the same way when he penned Psalm 18.

As I read this Psalm, I realize David has been on the run from Saul, with a group of 500 men in tow, adding to his stress. David did nothing wrong, yet Saul hunted him, desiring to do one thing; kill him.

The Psalms are full of David calling out to God for rescue from his enemies. Can you imagine trying to run from someone who is bent on ruthlessly killing you and all those traveling with you? The safety of everyone would weigh heavily on your mind. In addition, David had to feed these men and somehow keep them disciplined. David, at times, surely felt he was in over his head. Yet his eyes remained focused on the LORD.

When the LORD rescued David from Saul, David penned Psalm 18, I love how David describes in verse sixteen what the LORD did. He writes these words, "He reached down from on high and took hold of me; he drew me out of deep waters." David followed God's plan when the waters of life were ready to overwhelm Him and allowed God to rescue him.

When I am tired because of life's deep water and feel I can no longer stand, I need to keep my eyes forward on the LORD and allow Him to draw me out of deep water. Allowing God to rescue me involves deep trust in Him and a firm belief He knows what He is doing. I find when I allow Him to draw me out of deep water, I become refreshed, my strength to stand is renewed, and I can go forward with rekindled energy. If you are too tired to stand, if you are in deep water, why not let the God of all creation draw you out, help you up, and give you the strength to go forward?

Digging Deeper

1) Do you feel you are in deep water? Why or why not?
2) How will you turn your eyes and focus on God?
3) How can members of the group you are meeting with support you?

THE GRAPE WHINED

What did the grape do when he got stepped on?
He let out a little wine.

When I get stepped on in life, I have a tendency to whine. But in addition to whining, I find that getting stepped on raises trust issues for me. The trust issues are not just with the person who stepped on me, but the scars of being stepped on carry over to all other areas of my life that involve trust. I have found in order to avoid anything which may bump up against those trust scars, I strive to be perfect. The perfect leader, husband, father, small group leader, etc.

One of the results of living with this burden I have placed on myself is my tendency to defend myself against anything that could even be considered a mistake. This drives my friends, family, and co-workers up the wall. It's really difficult to provide constructive feedback to me when I constantly refuse to admit there is any need to improve.

I also know that I am not the only one who has this issue. So how do those of us with trust issues begin to step away from our carefully constructed defense of perfectionism? For me, the answer is to begin trusting the God who created this Universe. Notice I did not say I need to trust in him. I've done that and I know He is my Savior. I know he has forgiven my sins past, present, and future. Yet I find I do not trust Him to protect me from being misunderstood, from the guilt I feel when I am not perfect, or the ridicule I feel when others point out my mistakes.

This is a tension point for me. I do not trust that God is in control, especially during those times I feel like I have failed others or perceive that others have treated me like slime, even if they haven't. Yet at the point of tension, I have found that God is right beside me. I have found great help as I struggle to grasp how the Creator of all the Universe walks with me in my inability to trust Him. Proverbs 3:5-6 says, "Trust in the LORD with all your heart and do not lean on your own understanding. In all your ways submit to Him, and He will make your paths straight." In Hebrew the word LORD is Yahweh which means "He who created all things." The word "heart" in Hebrew is "leb" which means our inner essence. With those words understood, I recognize I am to trust the creator of all the things from within the inner essence of who I am.

I am in the midst of a journey in which I am learning to admit I'm not perfect. I know there will be times I will be misunderstood, or I misunderstand people's reaction to me, but at those times my goal is to trust Yahweh from the very depth of my being to help me work it all out. It isn't easy, but it has been an awesome journey so far. Why not join me?

Digging Deeper

1) All of us struggle to trust God in some area of life. What is yours?

2) As you begin to trust God in the area you just wrote down, how will you stay on this journey?
3) How can members of the group you are meeting with support you?

THE FUTURE, THE PRESENT, THE PAST

The future, the present, and the past all walked
into a bar.
Things got a little tense.

I wish I could say things never get a little tense for me,
but I would be lying. The truth is, things get tense for all of
us at times whether it is with our work, spouse, friends,
family or church. The question is what do we do during those
times of tension?

I find when I rely on myself to deal with a tense situation
I fail. When I pause, take a deep breath, focus on Christ, and
start praying, things turn out much better. That's not as easy
as it sounds. In fact, I find the process of taking a deep
breath, focusing on Christ, and praying to be an extremely
difficult process to complete when I am in the midst of a
crisis. I often find I have to go back, refocus, and go through
the entire process again and again.

Paul talks about doing this in Philippians 4:6 where he
writes, "Do not be anxious about anything, but in every
situation, by prayer and petition with thanksgiving, present
your requests to God." There are three points we need to
follow if we are not going to be anxious, especially in tense
situations. First, we need to dump all of our burdens on

44

Christ through prayer. I see this in the text when Paul writes, "…but in every situation by prayer…" In every situation or as the Greek translation states, "…in everything…" I am to pray. That is really hard for me to comprehend. Christ wants me to bring everything to Him. He wants me to bring my anger, even if it is at Him, my pain, my hurt, my sin, everything—and completely unload it all on Him. I have a difficult time with the thought that the God of all creation takes such a deep, personal interest in me. He wants me to dump all of those things which cause tension in my life on Him! Second, we are to engage in petition (praying earnestly). In the Greek language the word "petition" is tied to the verb "anxious." Anxious is in the active voice which means the action never stops. This means "petition" is also active because it is affected by the action of the verb anxious. Let me put that into plain English. We are to continually go back again and again to Christ in prayer with everything, even all those things I have already prayed about. Third, we need to accept the peace that Christ will bring to us. Sometimes we get comfortable with our tension and it's hard to let it go. Yet Christ's promise is that God's peace "…will guard our hearts and our minds in Christ Jesus." So, when tension invades your life, why not just dump it on Christ as many times as you need to, then accept His peace? I know from experience His peace does pass all understanding.

Digging Deeper

1) What tension do you struggle in giving and leaving with God?

2) What can you do to help you remember God wants you to continually bring your issues to Him?
3) How can members of the group you are meeting with support you?

BOILED WATER

R.I.P. boiled water, you will be mist.

When I read this pun, I immediately think of the Israelites and manna. Can you think of eating the same thing day in and day out, every day, year after year? Here is a conversation I imagine could have happened.

A curious voice asks, "Hey mom, what are we having for breakfast?"

Mom's short response is, "Manna."

Around lunch time a child hesitantly asks, "Mom, what's on the menu for lunch?"

The answer is spoken with in a tired flat tone, "It's going to be manna."

Then comes supper and the question, "Mom, it's almost time for supper, what the meal going to be?"

With an aggravated voice mom shouts back, "Still manna, now leave me alone!"

When I read about manna in Exodus 16:1-21, I notice the Israelites had a real issue in trusting God to provide for them. Verse twenty makes it clear that some people tried to gather more manna then they should have, only to have it turn foul and breed worms. It would be really easy to sit back in my chair and think, "Those Israelites were pretty stupid, after everything God did in Egypt for them, they still couldn't trust him." Yet if I'm honest I have to admit I am a lot like those Israelites. God has done so much for me in my life, yet at times I still struggle with believing he will provide for my needs in the future. I don't think I'm alone in this. We as humans find it difficult to trust an unseen God even though He has already proven how He can take care of us.

So, what is the solution? Let's go to an event in the New Testament with a strange conversation in Mark 9:24. Jesus, Peter, James, and John are returning from the Mount of Transfiguration. When they reach the disciples, a distraught father tells Jesus that his son is possessed with a spirit and the disciples can't cast it out. Jesus addresses the man in verse twenty-three, "Everything is possible for one who believes." The father responds in verse twenty-four with "…I do believe; help my unbelief." When I envision the father speaking, I see him point to his head and say "I do believe;" then he points to his heart and states "…help me overcome my unbelief!"

This is exactly what I need to do when I find it difficult to trust God. I need to say, "Father I believe, as I point to my head, please help my unbelief, as I point to my heart. In doing this I tell God I am trying to believe in my heart, yet I am struggling to do so. Every time I have prayed this earnestly, God has given me peace. Sometimes that peace is immediate and sometimes it is painfully slow in coming. But when it is slow in coming, I keep praying and find that although there is not peace, Christ is walking with me as I struggle.

Next time you are not sure if there will be manna tomorrow, why not stop, point to your head and earnestly tell God, "I believe," then point to your heart and say, "Help my unbelief." You will be amazed at what God will do.

Digging Deeper

1) Recount a time when you have struggled with believing God will provide what you need.
2) In the future, will praying about your "unbelief" help? Why or why not?
3) How can members of the group you are meeting with support you?

LETTUCE AND TOMATO

Did you hear about the race between the lettuce
and the tomato?
*The lettuce was a head and the tomato
was trying to ketchup.*

Have you ever felt you needed to catch up to other
people? Maybe they are athletic, dance better, or seem to
outshine you in some other way. I feel like that each time our
youngest daughter participates in an athletic event. Many of
the other moms and dads talk about their days in college
athletics and I am left feeling like someone who can't even
make the bench warming team. I have that feeling because
my eyes become focused on how I think the world perceives
me and not on how God identifies me.

In Psalm 139, David tells us how we are viewed by God.
In verse fourteen he writes, "I praise you because I am
fearfully and wonderfully made; your works are wonderful,
I know that full well." David has hit the nail squarely on the
head. God made us separately and unique, each having
different skills and talents. Yet each of us is wonderfully
made. God sees us as He made us, not as we see us. The next
time I start to compare myself to other people by this world's
standards I am going to turn to Psalm139, read it, and think

about how God views me. Let's take this step of spiritual growth together.

Digging Deeper

1) In what circumstances have you compared yourself to other people?
2) What is your spiritual gift and how do you use it?
3) List the talents God has given you.
4) How can members of the group you are meeting with support you?

ELEPHANTS IN TREES

Why do you never see elephants hiding in trees?
Because they are so good at it.

There are times that I feel God is like an elephant hiding in a tree, He's extremely good at hiding from me. I've struggled with that thought because I wonder what kind of a spiritual low life I am to entertain such thoughts. When I finally had the courage to share my feelings with others, it turns out most of them wrestle with the same feelings.

In Psalms 22:1-2, David talks about this. He writes, "My God, my God, why have you forsaken me? Why are you so far from saving me, so far from my cries of anguish?" In Hebrew this verse reads, "My God, my God, why have you forsaken me, (Why are you) so far from helping me…" Notice how David repeats himself twice. He uses "My God" twice in a row and then speaks to the distance between himself and God twice. Whenever a Jewish writer immediately repeats a word, phrase or thought, he is telling the reader what he has written is extremely important. This shouts to me that David is in anguish because he feels abandoned by God.

How does David handle this? When we read further in Psalm 22, we find David working through this tension point. In verses three through five, he states that God is holy. This is an admission that God is God and he is not. So, the first thing he does is humble himself, admit that he is not God, and acknowledge that God is holy. Next, he recounts how God has acted in the past. This focuses his mind on remembering how God has acted throughout his life. He ends verse five by talking about how the fathers of Israel trusted in God and were not disappointed. As the Psalm progresses, we see David struggle, but we also see how he constantly looks at who God is and what God has done. The end result is he praises and exalts God. How did David progress from believing God hid from him, to exalting God? The answer is this; David focused his mind on who God is and what He had done.

In this Psalm I see that even a person who has been called a man after God's own heart, felt that God was hiding from him just like I do at times. I also learned that when this happens, I need to refocus my thoughts from, "Where are you God?" to remembering all He has done for me. When I do this, I find that my LORD is where He has always been, standing right beside me.

Here is a challenge, when you feel God is hiding; grab some paper, then write down what God has done in the past. Then join David and me as we stand in awestruck wonder at our LORD who has never left our side.

Digging Deeper

1) Recall one time you felt God was hiding from you and share it with your group (make sure each member does this).

2) What steps will you take to refocus your thoughts when this happens again?
3) How can members of the group you are meeting with support you?

SUSHI

I would avoid the Sushi if I were you.
It's a little fishy.

If I were asked about sushi, I would emphatically declare DO NOT EAT IT! The thought of eating small pieces of raw fish mixed with vegetables and rice, wrapped in seaweed has no appeal. For me it's just stinky fish and rice, wrapped in some type of strange tasting non-animal substance that is repulsive. Trust me, if I was ever asked for guidance about eating sushi, I would let my feelings be made known. I would also have to be honest and say my repulsiveness is a personal opinion and not everyone would give the same advice.

The world is the same way. When we ask others for guidance regarding difficult events, we get varied answers. Those answers depend on the world view of the individual who is responding to the question. Some people will give ultra-conservative advice while others will provide an ultra-liberal view. Other individuals will provide a response from a world view somewhere in between the two. With so many world views speaking, how do we know who to turn to?

For me, this is where the Bible comes in. It is a book written through the span of fifteen centuries, by over forty authors, ranging from farmers to kings, in three different continents, during times of war, peace, great joy, anguish and suffering, and is composed in three different languages—Hebrew, Greek, and Aramaic. Yet it has one central theme, which is about the relationship between mankind and the only living God. As such I have come to trust it for guidance in the face of all other voices speaking to me.

I have found a lot of wisdom in the book of Proverbs. It gives me practical advice for dealing with life events. In chapter three, verses twenty-seven through thirty-one I am given a list which tells me how to be honest with others. To be honest this is not a favorite list, because there are times I really do not like what it says, but if I am searching for truth regarding being honest with others, this is where I will find it. Each statement in this list begins with a "do not."

There are two Hebrew words typically used for "do not," they are *Lo* and *Al*. Of the two, Al is emphatic. Think of someone holding the hand of a three-year-old toddler who they deeply love. Suddenly the toddler breaks away and runs out into a six-lane street during rush hour traffic. I'm pretty sure the person holding the toddler's hand would not gently say, "Oh, don't do that." I think the "don't do that" would be shouted at the top of the individual's lungs as panic set in and in an adrenaline-fueled sprint, raced to save the toddler from certain death. The word Al is used in this passage. It emphatically directs me to live my life a certain way, an honest way, a way that is different from the world I live in. I hate this passage because there are times in my life, I don't want to be honest with my neighbor and I want to withhold good from others. Yet the guidance here is unmistakable. I need to do these things to live a life of honesty. This is a challenge for me, and for most of us. Let's do this together.

Digging Deeper

1) Read Proverbs 3:27-31. Which one of these do you struggle with? Why?
2) What are some steps you can take to help you live out these verses?
3) How can members of the group you are meeting with support you?

BURNING BROWNIES

I just burned 2,000 calories.
That's the last time I leave brownies in the oven
while I nap.

I've never burned brownies because I've napped. Popcorn yes, brownies no. The sad thing is, I've done that more than once. You'd think I would learn my lesson the first time and not nap when I put popcorn on the stove top. I experience the same thing with sin. I should learn my lesson the first time and not put myself in a situation which leads to my act of sin. Yet I find that I place myself in that position and end up sinning again and again and again. I don't think I'm alone in this struggle. Many of us fight temptation, yet at some point we give in to the same sin, again and again and again.

I wonder if anyone feels the same way I do when I end up repeating the same sin over and over again? Do we feel worthless, inadequate, or hopeless? When I look at my repetitive sin, I often feel like I am a fake Christian, unable to live a Godly life. It seems that there is no hope for me. Yet the Bible shows me differently.

I am glad the Bible never hides the faults of some of its heroes. One of those heroes is the apostle Paul. He steadfastly served God through hardships and trials. Even when he was thrown in prison, he sang praises to God. Yet in Romans 7:15 he tells us that he does not do the thing that he wants but instead he does the very thing that he hates. Next, in verse eighteen he states, "For I know that good itself does not dwell in me, that is, in my sinful nature. For I have the desire to do what is good, but I cannot carry it out." Then in verse twenty-four it seems that he screams out in agony these words, "What a wretched man I am! Who will rescue me from this body that is subject to death?"

I love seeing this human side of Paul. It seems that he is right beside me feeling inadequate and worthless. But look at what happens when we follow the text into chapter eight. Paul shows us that there is hope, not just hope, but resolution to our consistently doing those things which we hate to do. The first verse of Romans chapter eight tells us, "There is therefore now no condemnation for those who are in Christ Jesus." Let me state that again. There is no condemnation for those who are in Christ Jesus. This means those of us who earnestly struggle against temptation and sin, but fail, like Paul, are not condemned. The blood of Jesus Christ covers our sin.

Because I am a child of God covered by the blood of Jesus, I have hope even though I constantly repeat my sin. Do you have the hope provided by Christ? If your answer is no, why not invite Christ to come into your heart, cover you with His blood, and forgive your sins? Then grasp hold of the hope that only He can offer.

Digging Deeper

1) Do you struggle with the idea that because of repetitive sin, you are a fake Christian, or not of value to God.
2) Does reading about how Pauls regards himself help you to understand that you are not worthless but are of great value to God?
3) When you read Romans 8:1 in conjunction with chapter 7:14-25, does it help? Why or why not?
4) How can members of the group you are meeting with support you?

SKYDIVING SEEING EYE

Why don't blind people sky dive?
Because it makes their dogs extremely anxious.

I have no doubt that a seeing eye dog could be trained to skydive, although I have never seen one do so. However, I have seen pictures of armed forces dogs sky diving. These courageous animals are held to their handlers by a special harness. There is a reason for the harness. You see although the dog is free falling, she is not a skydiver. The dog needs someone who is in control in order to survive. Could you imagine what would happen if the dog was in control of the free fall? Would she know how to correct a spin or maneuver herself? Would she be able to safely land herself and her handler in a safe landing zone?

Sometimes I feel I am the same way with God. I often find myself taking control of my life and trying to guide myself to a safe landing zone. However, He sees our lives from beginning to end and knows how to get us to a safe landing zone. The translators of the NIV Bible write this in Psalms 139:16, "Your eyes saw my unformed body; all the days ordained for me were written in your book before one of them came to be." When I try to take control of my life, I place myself above God and tell Him I'm wiser than He is.

I find Proverbs chapter thirty helps me when I do this. This chapter reminds me that I am not God. Verse four reads, "Who has gone up to heaven and come down? Whose hands have gathered up the wind? Who has wrapped up the waters in a cloak? Who has established all the ends of the earth? What is his name, and what is the name of his son? Surely you know!" Am I able to descend in and out of heaven, gather the wind in my hand, wrap up the waters in a cloak, or establish all the ends of the earth? The obvious answer is no. Yet God can and has done all these things.

Knowing what He has done, and what I can't do, takes me back to the image of a dog controlling a free fall; it's a disaster just waiting to happen. When I take control of my life's decisions and believe I know more than God, it's a disaster just waiting to happen. The wise thing to do is to let God have full control and guide me to where He knows I should be. Why not join me in admitting we are lousy at making life's decisions on our own and asking God to take control?

Digging Deeper

1) Describe a time in your life that you took control of a life decision instead of letting God guide and direct you. What happened? How did it turn out?
2) How will you use Proverbs 30 to lean on when you recognize you are beginning to replace God?
3) How can members of the group you are meeting with support you?

PRIEST TO LAWYER

What do you call a priest who becomes a lawyer?
A father-in-law.

My in-laws are citizens of a different country. They speak English far better than I speak their native tongue, yet they are hesitant to do so because they believe they would mistakenly say something offensive. Yet when I interact with them, their actions toward me convey their acceptance of me. They call me brother and bend over backwards to show I am accepted. Their behavior has caused me to consider my actions toward others.

Do I treat others in the same manner my in-laws treat me? Sadly, I would have to admit my answer is no. When I think of what I should do, I am reminded of how John talks about Jesus as he faced this very issue. The story is in the fourth chapter of the gospel of John. Let me explain what is going on. Jesus is traveling from Judea to Galilee and has to pass through Samaria. To the Jews, the people of Samaria were scum, lower than dirt, not worthy of being spoken to or interacted with unless needed. Jesus is weary from his journey and sits by Jacob's well. The disciples had left to go buy food in the city, leaving Jesus all alone. A woman approaches the well and Jesus asks, "Will you give me a drink?" Let's put this in perspective. Jesus addresses a woman in a society that considered women beneath notice, who is from a people group the Jews consider to be scum. Then He asks for a drink. Think about that. Jesus had nothing to drink with, so the woman would have had to give Him a drink using her own ladle or at least using the bucket she was carrying. This means that Jesus' lips would have touched the ladle or the bucket's edge this women's lips touched. The woman is astounded and in verse nine asks Jesus, "…'How can you ask me for a drink?' (For Jews do not associate with Samaritans." (John 4:9) As we read through the story, we see that Jesus offers her living water.

Jesus is concerned for the soul of this woman. He sees her as a person who needs what He is offering, not as some worthless scum. The disciples come back and are amazed He was speaking with a woman. Do you see the difference here? Jesus reaches out to the scorned and rejected, while the disciples are wondering why He would do such a thing.

This story convicts me every time I read it. I have to ask myself who I am more like, Jesus or the disciples. Every time I ask myself that question, I have to hang my head and admit that I am far more like the disciples. This year, one of my goals is to reach out to those who society says are untouchable. I want to be more like Jesus, not the disciples. Would you join me?

Digging Deeper

1) What people group cause you to be more like the disciples (e.g. drunks, the homeless, LGBTQ, etc.)?

2) What will you do to minister to this group during this year? Describe your actions.
3) How can members of the group you are meeting with support you?

SOCCER

I don't play soccer because I enjoy the sport.
I'm doing it for kicks.

Our daughter played soccer until she reached third grade and then decided that basketball was the sport she wanted to focus on. I enjoyed watching her play, but I never enjoyed it enough to play it, especially to play just for kicks.

I have found in my spiritual life there are times I love to dwell on negative things. When I do this, I get a kick from it. I dwell on perceived insults, failures, and feeling of inadequacy. When I do this, I produce some very un-Christian thoughts.

The writer of Proverbs thirty speaks to this in verse thirty-three when he writes, "For as churning cream produces butter, and as twisting the nose produces blood, so stirring up anger produces strife." The word "churning" and "pressing" is the same Hebrew word, *mits*. Using *mits* twice is the author's way of emphasizing his point. This verse tells me that if I dwell on the negative—the wrongdoing I perceive others have done to me, failures, guilt, or feelings of inadequacy—strife will follow.

The other side of the coin is to discipline myself to think a different way. This way of thinking is not easy. Yet I find comfort with what Paul writes in Philippines 3:13-14.

66

"Brothers and sisters, I do not consider myself yet to have taken hold of it. But one thing I do: Forgetting what is behind and straining toward what is ahead, I press on toward the goal to win the prize for which God has called me heavenward in Christ Jesus." The words I need to focus on here are in verse fourteen, "Forgetting what is behind and straining toward what is ahead…" If I dwell on what lies ahead for me in Christ Jesus, I forget what lies behind. I forget the supposed insults, failure, guilt, and feelings of inadequacy and instead focus on the mercy, love, and forgiveness of what Christ gives to me. This allows me to make the past, the past, and press forward to whatever God may offer. Although this is not easy it is rewarding because of the peace it brings. I'm committed to forgetting the past and pressing forward. Join me, and together we can forget the past as we press forward into what God offers.

Digging Deeper

1) What is one event you constantly think about which brings about strife for you? Does it deal with supposed insults, failure, guilt inadequacy, or something else? Please explain.
2) Focusing on God instead of what lies in the past will probably mean stepping outside of your comfort zone. Who will you ask to help you as you begin this journey?
3) How can members of the group you are meeting with support you?

NOAH MAKING COFFE

How does Noah make coffee?
Hebrews it.

Hebrews chapter eleven is often times referred to as the Hall of Faith. In the text we find Noah, Abraham, Jacob, Moses, and David to name a few. As I review Noah's life, I find that after building the ark, enduring the raging storm which flooded the earth, then waiting until the land was dry and God said to leave the ark, Noah blew it. In Genesis chapter 9:20-21 we read this, "Noah, a man of the soil, proceeded to plant a vineyard. When he drank some of its wine, he became drunk and lay uncovered inside his tent." This righteous man (Genesis 6:9) got drunk, naked, and passed out in view of anyone who happened to pass by his tent. He blew it!

Have you ever blown it? I have. I remember watching our daughter play in a basketball tournament. There was a mom from the other team whose chair was bumped up against mine. On every play, she screamed into my ear. I put up with it as long as I could then I asked her to stop, she told me to get over it, I was at a sporting event. I became furious. I went after her, yelling and screaming into her ear every chance I got. It was very obvious to everyone what I was doing and I continued doing it even when she got red in the face, crossed her arms, and became quiet. I brought shame to myself, to my wife, my daughter, and her team. Oh, did I mention my daughter plays for a faith-based team?

My shame over my actions continues to overwhelm me. Yet when I read the eleventh chapter of Hebrews, I realize I am in good company. We have already seen Noah's failure. Then there is Abraham, who twice lied about Sarah being his wife just to save his own skin. Moses, the guy who killed an Egyptian and had to make a run for it across the desert, is also listed in this chapter. Who can forget David, who committed adultery then had Bathsheba's husband killed? How could each of those men be counted as Biblical heroes? It's because God, in His mercy and grace forgave them just as He forgives us.

One of Christ's disciples, John, wrote a series of letters. In 1 John 1:8-9 he writes about God's forgiveness. Verse eight states, "If we claim to be without sin, we deceive ourselves and the truth is not in us." Notice the use of the word "we." John is plainly stating that everyone, including himself, sins. If you say you don't you are a lair. So how do we receive forgiveness? John gives us the answer in verse nine. "If we confess our sins, he is faithful and just and will forgive us our sins and purify us from all unrighteousness." Notice the word "all." That's inclusive, it means everything! Look at this promise. If I have accepted within the very core of my being that Christ is my Lord and my Savior and has forgiven my sins, then I go to Him in humbleness and ask for forgiveness for everything I have done wrong He will forgive me.

Dealing with shame means I accept God's forgiveness and allow myself to move on. For me, I have accepted God's forgiveness for the basketball incident. Each time we watch my daughter's team play, I remember what I did, but not with shame. Instead, God's forgiveness allows me to let the past strengthen me and provide wisdom for the present and the future. So today why not accept the forgiveness provided by God that John talks about, and allow the past to give you the wisdom for the present and the future?

Digging Deeper

1) What incident or actions from the past haunt you? Please explain.
2) What is holding you back from accepting Christ's forgiveness and moving on?
3) How can members of the group you are meeting with support you?